A Context for a Renewed Economics

A Context
for a
Renewed Economics

MICHAEL SPENCE

With an introduction by

DAVID MITCHELL

Waldorf
PUBLICATIONS

Published by:

Waldorf Publications at the
Research Institute for Waldorf Education
38 Main Street
Chatham, NY 12037

Title: *A Context for a Renewed Economics*
Author: Michael Spence
Editor: David Mitchell
Layout: Ann Erwin

First printed in 1990
© 2014 by Waldorf Publications
ISBN # 978-1-936367-66-5

*The four lectures contained in this booklet were delivered
to the Association of Waldorf Schools of North America
Economic Conference on November 17 & 18, 1989, in Fair Oaks, CA.
They are lectures and should be read as such.
The contents have not been revised by the lecturer.*

Contents

A Historical Perspective on Financing Waldorf Schools[*]

David Mitchell

As the decade of the nineties begins, we observe a political world that is undergoing profound change. The Berlin Wall, a symbol of repression for three decades, is being torn apart and sold in pieces by enterprising agents of the capitalistic West. Communist dogma is being abandoned because of the abstractness of its philosophical concepts and its resultant inability to bring about healthy economic growth and stability. This failure and the subsequent explosion with which change has occurred has everyone holding his breath. What will happen next?

As freedom becomes a reality for the Eastern Bloc, word reaches us that a Waldorf school is already on the drawing board for Budapest, and one suspects that Moscow may not be far behind. However, here in North America our Waldorf schools are increasingly threatened because the financial foundations of many schools are not as strong as they should be. In the light of world events and the excitement of change, can we, as administrators and teachers within Waldorf schools, re-examine our thinking as to how our schools are financially structured?

---

[*]This introduction and these lectures, all from 1989, were written before the dissolution of the USSR and before significant facts concerning the founding of the first Waldorf school were discovered (see *The Multifaceted Life of Emil Molt*, Waldorf Publications, 2012).

To begin with, we might look at the historical evolution of our Waldorf schools and the political circumstances that attended their birth 70 years ago.

The first major disaster in this century was World War I. Europe was devastated. For the first time the world's major nations, as allies, were involved in an all-against-all conflict. It was thought then to be a war to end all wars. A new time was heralded. Many Germans were particularly concerned and awakened a feeling of responsibility. Some were asking questions and earnestly seeking answers to what had gone wrong socially that could produce such a confrontation in a modern technologically advanced state.

One of these concerned individuals was Emil Molt, the owner of the Waldorf Astoria factory in Stuttgart. Molt felt that industrialists should accept the challenge and the responsibility to initiate change. He believed that new social alternatives were needed both to heal the damage caused by the war and to pave the way for the dawning of a new social consciousness.

With a group of friends he attempted political reform, recognizing the fundamental need for spiritual freedom, equality of rights, and economic brotherhood. This tripartite social organization was called the Threefold Social Order by its originator, an Austrian philosopher named Dr. Rudolf Steiner.

An offspring of this initiative was Molt's interest in education. He felt that if children could receive a balanced and harmonious education based on a comprehensive picture of man, then they might be better prepared for this new way of thinking that he felt was necessary to deal with modern world problems.

Because the German post-war government was made subservient under the Treaty of Versailles, it became unfeasible to discuss the realization of the Threefold Social Order further. Nearly every aspect of the new government was proscribed from without, and few were interested in concepts of government from within a defeated country. Thus Molt's interest in education took on a new dimension in the face of political realities.

Molt called upon Karl Stockmeyer, a leading anthroposophist, and asked him to start a school for children of the workers of his factory in Stuttgart. In a reply to this request Stockmeyer began to work out the basic elements of a school. Together they had certain principles they wished to see embodied.

> The school must be a germ for a really comprehensive school—financing must be raised out of free gifts. School fees would not properly correspond to the sense of our striving. In their place would be a kind of self-taxation by the parent community. The school itself would be a cooperation of teachers; that is, the teachers would have a hand in the entire administration and business life of the school, including the financial administration. A parent advisory council would be created through which the wishes of the parents could find their representation. As a representative body of the parents, it would have access to the school business and administration. The school's curriculum and internal working including the method of teaching would be handled within, by the teachers. Everything of a sectarian nature must be avoided.[1]

Molt had wanted, at first, for Stockmeyer to take over directorship of the school, but on April 23, 1919, he offered it to Dr. Rudolf Steiner in a meeting attended by Molt, Steiner, Stockmeyer, and Herbert Hahn. On this occasion Molt pronounced the name "Free Waldorf School" for the first time. By this word "Free" he meant a spiritually free school, open to anyone. He asked Steiner questions such as: How might a curriculum be formed to meet these goals of developing a "total education" for the complex life of the 20th and 21st centuries?

Waldorf education was therefore based upon Rudolf Steiner's world outlook and on his observations and conclusions about the nature of the human being. Steiner rejected the modern materialistic view of man so prevalent in Western society, and held that man, rather than being a purely mechanically functioning physical being, has spiritual aspects as well that must be vigorously nurtured during childhood if the creative capacities of the adult were to be expected to function fully. He saw a deeply rooted relationship between the physical being of man and the spiritual being of man. Between these two poles lies the soul, which surrounds and binds together both the physical and the spiritual.

Molt bought "Uhlandshohe," a restaurant near a stone quarry on a hill overlooking the city of Stuttgart. Initially he wanted the restaurant renovated to accommodate both a school and a children's home, but soon saw that both would not be possible at that time.

Steiner gave Stockmeyer the task of traveling about to gather an ensemble of teachers. He did this from June 26 until July 14, 1919. From August 27 until September 7, 1919, Steiner gave a number of lectures to these first teachers and developed the curriculum of the school.

The property was secured on July 1, but when Steiner visited on July 17, the renovation had still not begun. On July 23 the masons arrived, but the building was infested with bugs and had to be fumigated before work could proceed. With many obstacles overcome, and a lot of breaths being held, the building was finally ready for the first classes of children in September. Imagine that! An entire school of considerable size was staffed and prepared in a little more than three months!

Tuition was free for the children of the workers of the Waldorf Astoria factory. Others who wished to attend the school made a contribution of their own reckoning. Financial issues at that time were still relatively simple. The major costs were covered by Molt and his factory.

The high ideals of the Waldorf School necessitated that there be a proper relationship between the parents, for whom the original school was founded, and the teachers who were to pour their life-blood into its workings.

A major step in that direction occurred when Molt's firm gave way to an association in which parents and teachers joined. This association was also opened to friends and supporters from throughout the world; it guided the delicate undertaking of the school through the dangerous times of post-war inflation and terrible unemployment. Even though many people made sacrifices during these times, it was Molt's support that provided the needed financial stability. He involved his firm so deeply in the financial support of the school that the company lost ground against its competitors. The Waldorf School remained, but the Waldorf Astoria Factory fell into other hands. Molt was very clear about which was the most important initiative to be rescued. From that point on, the fiscal health of the school relied upon parent and state support.

Waldorf education is today the leading independent school movement in the world with schools in nearly every non-Communist country. There are over 400 schools worldwide and more than 100 here in North America.*

In November 1989, the Association of Waldorf Schools of North America sponsored two conferences entitled "The Context for a Renewed Economics." The first conference was held at the Pine Hill Waldorf School in Wilton, NH. The second took place at the Sacramento Waldorf School in Fair Oaks, CA. At these conferences approximately 150 individuals gathered to hear a series of talks by Michael Spence from Emerson College in Forest Row, England. Mr. Spence has, for many years, worked with the social, economic, and legal thoughts which were alive at the founding of the first Waldorf School in Stuttgart. The following lectures bring these ideas to life in our time.

---

*At the time of this printing, there are over 1000 schools worldwide and more than 165 schools and institutes in North America, according to the Freunde der Erziehungskunst.

The Threefold Nature of Social Life

Michael Spence

I must say with this visit to America, first in New Hampshire and now here in Fair Oaks, I find it immensely encouraging to find so many people who are wanting to work with these questions of the threefold social order in one way or another. If we look at the development of the work since Rudolf Steiner's time, if we look at the teaching, at the arts, and eurythmy, and so forth, we see a tremendous amount of effort and tremendous development. And, if we look in the spheres of economics, of administration, et cetera, in which we really hope to be looking at here, you will find only comparatively recently an increase in activity. By and large, when it comes to an understanding of the threefold nature of social life, we are still asleep. In most of the institutions we are still asleep, and so I find it very heartening that people are beginning to ask questions and beginning to want really to bring, I hope, something into their schools, and so on. So I will try to contribute at least something towards that work, towards that development.

Today I was going to try to give a little bit of a picture of this threefold nature of social life. It's really not something that is easy to grasp fully. It takes time. It takes work. I know many of you will have already been working at this and will already have more or less an understanding of it. Tomorrow I hope to bring a little bit more about how one can begin to work with these ideas in our institutions, in our schools, colleges, and so forth, how we can begin to work in some of the questions arising. I know many of you have questions, and I have a horrible feeling some of you think that I'm going to be able to answer your problems. Actually, I hope that when we leave tomorrow, you will have more questions than when you started. Then I feel we will have gotten somewhere.

Now, in studying this social question, there are a number of points I'd like to bring out because I think there are many misunderstandings. I tend to use the term the threefold nature of social life. I don't always use it, as I don't believe that one should always stick to one term. But nevertheless, I believe this term simply leads one to a truer understanding of it. We talk about the threefold nature of the human being, and one tries to come an understanding of the threefold nature from the teacher, the doctor, the nutritionist, for examples. One has to try to come to an understanding of this threefold nature. It is there. In a social life, it's really the same thing: There is a threefold nature. It's not something that's imposed on us, or if we divide it into three, it would work out nicely. It's actually got a threefold nature. Now our question is: How do we begin to perceive this and then form our institutions out of the very nature of social life? If one uses the term threefold social order, it always gives a picture of imposing an order onto something rather than finding the form that arises out of it.

It's very interesting that I had a certain problem for many years when people talked about the middle sphere, and it was actually when I was reading something of Rudolf Steiner as he talked about the threefold nature of the four seasons, that suddenly something became available to me. The polarities between winter and summer and then spring and autumn in a way are the same. They are both moving between these two. The polarity is that they're moving in opposite directions. And suddenly this sort of form implied a different way, gave me a picture of a fourfold nature of the threefold nature of social life, but I'll come to that a bit later.

I find wide misunderstanding where people often fail to distinguish something, and I'll try and make that clear; but before I do that, I just want to say one thing. In these social questions, there's no person who knows the answers. You always find that one begins to come to an understanding when people work together. So I'm fully aware that I bring several points to which other people might disagree, and I would disagree with them, but the truth will ultimately be found between us, not in any one. But it's very necessary that sometimes there are different viewpoints.

Nevertheless, I think it's important to distinguish something, and to be careful to always put the threefold natures into diagrammatic form. It's very easy to take the threefold natures and sort of string them all together. You see there is a threefold nature if the human being stands on one side, there are the kingdoms of nature beneath him—the animal world, the plant world, the mineral world that stand beneath him. Then there is the whole, you could say, of humanity itself, of mankind itself. And then there are the hierarchies which rise above the human being. Here you get the threefolds: The human being relates to the spiritual, the hierarchies; the human being relates to other human beings; and the human being has a relationship to the kingdoms of nature. That is one, so to speak, threefold relationship. It's very easy to mix that up with the threefold nature of social life.

In social life, we're really talking about the relationship of the individual human being to the whole of society. And also you take the threefold nature of the human being, when one talks about body, soul and spirit. Here again, it makes a very nice picture to say body, soul and spirit: economic life, the rights life (but that's a bit awkward so one calls it a social life), and spiritual life/cultural life. And this again can be extremely misleading, because if one talks about the realm of the state, so to speak, the realm of rights life being the realm of the state, and you put the soul into that, you should say that the government has control of the soul of the human being, and this leads to extraordinary distortion. So one has to be very careful of these threefoldnesses and trying to put them together in lovely diagrams.

Now another thought which I think is very important. Rudolf Steiner spoke a great deal, immediately at the end of the World War I and for a year or two after it, in 1919, about this whole threefold nature of social life, the Threefold Commonwealth. He gave many public lectures, wrote articles, met politicians, and tried to bring something new about. There was utter chaos in Europe after that first World War. Then at a certain point he stopped. The old thoughts had taken hold again. He hoped something new could come about, but the old thoughts had taken hold. He said something during a lecture on the seasons. (The lecture had nothing to do with this question; he just sort of put in a certain thought.) He said that he had to stop talking about this threefold commonwealth because he could perceive that the Michaelic thought had not yet entered deeply enough into mankind. Not even amongst a few people. (By that, I always felt he meant not even amongst the anthroposophists themselves.)

So then the question was for me, and I have lived with it for a long time, what is this Michaelic thought that had not entered into mankind, and has it entered now? Until it entered into humanity, we couldn't really even grasp this whole question of the threefold nature of social life. I'm quite convinced in my own mind, and from my own observations, that this Michaelic thought has entered now into many people, into a wide area of our community, particularly amongst the younger people. It is really connected with the way we perceive the other person.

How do we perceive the other person? When we meet another person—we go into the streets and we meet another person, or we go into a shop and we meet the shopkeeper. What do we see? Whom do we see? First of all I think we see, you could say, the uniform. Whether it's an actual uniform or the clothes they wear, we see their outer image. And to that, we put a label. They are a shopkeeper, a policeman, a teacher, or whatever. So we already label them by the outer garments, by their job, their place in life. We give them a certain character. We label them and that becomes what we see. But beyond all that, what is there? Beyond the job, beyond the clothes, beyond the situation into which that person is born. Where is the individuality? Where is the unique being of that person, the divine spark? That we have to learn to see. To recognize that when we stand before another person, we stand before, in a certain sense, a being, a spiritual being who has been born into a physical body at birth, will leave that spiritual body behind at death, and will go on to new incarnations. We actually stand before a spiritual being. When one can awaken to that as a reality, then this whole question of a threefold nature of social life will become alive.

Now, I'd just like to characterize these three spheres. I think one can only characterize them in certain ways, just to get pictures; but one needs to work at these things time and time again so that they become quite clear, quite obvious to us. I can do it in this way, a way that I use often.

If we look at ourselves sitting here in this hall, each one of you is sitting separately, individually. Now, first of all, as you sit here, each of you, in your own way, carries your own thoughts. And as I speak, each of you actually responds in a slightly different way. What I say conjures up different pictures, different thoughts in you. In each one of you, it's different. Each one of you is unique and individual, and how you receive what I say depends on many things. It can depend, of course, particularly on your own being—that which you've brought to earth with you as your intentions, your qualities, your characteristics, your abilities. It can also be colored, so to speak, by the situation into which you are born, the culture into which you were born. But it's still unique; it's what you make of yourself.

You'll also experience in this realm (this place, you could say, in which you live as an individual being) the loneliness. You have an experience: I might say something, hopefully, or you see something, you read something, that lights up the truth to you, and suddenly you experience a moment of truth, of profound beauty. We all occasionally have these experiences which excite us. There's a question we've been working with, and suddenly something is revealed, and then one wants to share this thought, this truth. And you find you can't put it into words. You can't share it. Even with someone very close to you. We all have these times, times when we experience absolute loneliness, something of an experience we can't share. And this is also characteristic of what we call the cultural life, that in which our demand of society is freedom. The freedom to be ourselves, to develop the capacities we've brought with us. The freedom to find that task which we have set ourselves pre-birth. We need to find within our society this whole freedom.

If I spoke in such a way that you began to sense I was being rather clever and manipulating what I said so that it had an unconscious influence on you, I'd think, I'd hope, that you'd get very angry and walk out of the room because I was not leaving you free. It's very important that I speak in such a way that it leaves you absolutely free to accept it or not accept it—to make of it what you need to make of it. Your cultural life in the sphere of education, or religion, arts, everything that arises out of the inner nature of the human being, the creative capacity of the human being (you could say the super-sensible aspect of the human being) must be free. And that is what we refer to, you could say, as cultural-spiritual life.

Perhaps I can put it another way. Some of you might well have read different biographies, but there is one I read some years ago which moved me greatly. That is the biography of Anwar Sadat, the former president of Egypt, who was assassinated some years ago. His biography is called *In Search of Identity*. A very interesting title. In search of identity. Who am I? For a certain period in his early adult life, he was in prison. He was in prison in Egypt under the influence of the British, who then controlled Egypt to a large extent. He was a bit of a rebel fighting for independence, so he was imprisoned. We've all had this habit of putting these people in prison at times. It was very interesting.

In this prison, he was in solitary confinement for a while. We all know other people who have been through this experience. You can imagine, in prison you are physically enclosed. Your rights are taken away from you. You cannot get out. But in your inner being, you can still, so to speak, reach out. During this period he came to a tremendous revelation, a tremendous perception. He reached out and came to a certain understanding, a certain recognition, of his own identity and his relationship to the divine. He came to that in his struggles in this loneliness of the prison.

So who was this being; what was that in him that could reach beyond the prison bars and come to a certain identity, to a recognition of his own identity and his relationship to his God? He then expanded this when he became president to find the identity of the Egyptian people. It was largely in that search that he went to war with Israel really to find the identity of the Egyptian people. And then, he went beyond that. He found the identity of humanity. He discovered that despite all religions, ultimately, every human being reached up to the divine. Every human being, he perceived, reached to the divine. In that, all humanity was equal. Those weren't quite his words, but that was the idea, and so at that point—when he recognized the identity of humanity—he could meet the Jews and go to Israel to try to bridge that gap. This search of identity is the *cultural-spiritual life*.

Now let's look at a different aspect. Each of you is sitting on a different chair, and as you came into this room, you went and sat on an empty chair. None of you, I presume, pushed someone off the chair because that's what you wanted to sit on, or had an argument about it, or fought over it. You sat on an empty chair. Why? Why did you sit on an empty chair? What is that in our society that brings a certain form that says that if there's someone sitting on a chair, you don't come and sit on the same chair? You get another one. It's a sort of mutual understanding. It's something that just lives in this society, a certain form. Here we're touching on the rights life. This sphere of the rights life, sphere of state, sphere of law, the sphere, you could say, of good manners, in which every human being really is treated equally. This is where the individual demands of society that he be treated equally with every other human being. That which arises out of common opinion, in a certain sense, is the *rights sphere.*

I'll be talking more about this later, but perhaps I could bring one or two examples. I was looking at a notice the other day—you have more of them here, I think, than we have in England. You go out walking along the road, and you might want to stop and walk into the woods, but there's a notice which says, "Private. Keep Out. No Trespassing." So you stop. What is it then that actually stops you? Why do you pay attention to this notice? What is that notice? And why do you not continue forward? After all, it's only a bit of paper, a bit of writing on paper. Next, for example, you're driving along and you come to a traffic light and the light goes red and everybody stops. What brings them to a stop? Why does one stop when the light goes red? This is the realm of law. Something that we've created, so to speak, to bring ordering into our lives. It's very interesting. I have seen this notice in America—No Trespassing. Here, as I understand it, that is enforceable by law, and if you trespass, it is an offense. You will find the same notice in England, but behind it used to be no law; it was no offense. There was no such law, but actually in the last few years, they've just begun bringing in a law, so it now is. You once were free to walk on God's earth, so to speak. If you did any damage or caused a nuisance, that was an offense. Or if the farmer told you to leave and you refused, that was an offense. But not the walking itself. But even in different lands, different countries, the law changes. This is a sphere of law, a sphere in which we demand to be equal. When that light goes red, it applies to all people.

Now there's another aspect of your sitting here. You're each sitting on a chair because while you want to listen to me, you need to put your body somewhere. You want to put your body into a situation of rest, and you cannot float. In your physical body, you are subject to the physical laws, gravity, and so on, so you have to put your body in a chair to keep it comfortable. You've clothed it, you've fed it, you've brought it here. You've put it in a chair. Everything that relates to the physical body, everything that relates to the fact that between birth and death we live in physical bodies and because of that, we need the substance of the earth—all the activity, all that human activity that goes to providing these needs is what we call *economic life*.

Now we have again to be very careful, for if one in normal life talks of economic life, most of us think of money. If we think of whether something is economical, we think: Does it make a profit? But to get back to what I would say is the true reality, I sit on a chair, not on the money nor the monetary value of the chair. It's the chair I sit on. We do not survive on the money. We survive on that which is created by human labor, not the money, itself. It's very important to understand this.

When I use the term economic life, I'm referring to that activity which goes to providing our needs that arise because we have physical bodies. Now look at these needs; look at what you have, even just here: One has a chair, you're wearing clothes, most of you have paper, books, pencil. In this room at the moment, we need lights; we use electric lights. You've used motor cars to come here. You've just recently had a meal, no doubt. Think of all this and then ask yourself the question: How much of this did you, yourself, produce? How much of all this did you, yourself, produce for yourself? You'll come to the realization that in most cases, nothing at all. You didn't produce any of it. Some of you might have produced a bit of it. Just a little. But if you think what you need to live, you'll realize that you produce none of it yourself, or practically none. If you work in modern economic life, if you work in, let us say, the center, the core of modern economic life, the factories and industry, there you will find thatn practically everything you produce, you, yourself, do not use. Everything you produce goes to other people.

Here we find this characteristic of economic life: We're actually dependent on each other. No one produces, so to speak, for himself, or if he does, it's only minimal. For what I have, I am absolutely depended on the community; and what I produce, if I do produce, goes out to the community. Here, out of economic life itself arises the demand for brotherhood, for working for each other. If one had time really to study pure economics, leaving out morality and everything, you'd find one arrives at this point where brotherhood, altruism, is a necessity of economic life. The more altruism enters in, the more efficient the economy becomes, and this is a feature of economic life.

As an illustration: Yesterday morning I phoned my wife in England. Many of you, of course, are constantly on the phone. You phone someone perhaps at a great distance. Pick the telephone up, dial, eight, ten numbers, press ten digits, or twirl the thing around and wait sometimes for only a very, very short time, a matter of seconds—and suddenly you'll hear a ringing and you know there, 10,000 miles away, there's a bell ringing. Then she answers the phone, and you speak for a few minutes, and you put the phone down. How much does that cost? Not very much, a few dollars. The average person can earn a few dollars in a half hour, quarter of an hour, ten minutes; so with ten minutes' work, you have been able to create the possibility of speaking to someone 10,000 miles away. Yet if you look at what is involved in your phoning, what actually was brought into activity by your dialing, you find all that electronic equipment, all those cables that lie across the countryside, or the beaming up to the radio towers which send the signal across the country, or into the satellites high up, and then across the Atlantic Ocean. Now it goes two ways across the Atlantic Ocean. One is a cable that goes right across the Atlantic on the ocean bed, and the chances are if you speak on the phone, your voice is carried right underneath the ocean, right across the Atlantic. Then there are generating stations. The electricity has to be generated, so there are power stations which have to transfer your voice right across that area, and then the other one back. All this activity comes into being every time you make a phone call, and it costs you a few pence, and you think of the thousands and thousands of people involved—just in your speaking for five minutes to someone some distance away. There are thousands and thousands of people who were involved to make that possible. This again is a feature of economic life.

In economic life we can talk only about a world community. We cannot talk about any other community. There is no such thing as self-sufficiency. It's an illusion. In the world of cultural life we stand alone. But this is, so to speak, characteristic of these three spheres: In *economic life*, I depend on the community to provide my needs. In *rights life* I demand to be treated as an equal in bringing form and order into our society. And in the *cultural life*, I really need freedom to be myself, to develop my own capacities.

Now I'd just like to look at this from a different aspect. Last year at this time, my wife and I were in Australia. Our daughter immigrated down there. We'd given some lectures, particularly my wife had given some lectures, so we decided to treat ourselves. In Sydney there's one of those restaurants which is on top of a very tall tower and it revolves. You might have experienced one of these. It's a lovely one in Sydney; it's on a bit of a hill so it's really high up. It must be one of the tallest buildings in Sydney. We got a very good seat right by the window, and during dinner we went round more than one and a bit times and completely saw the whole of Sydney as the sun slowly set. Looking down on Sydney, I tried to say: What am I seeing? What do I see? Below—all the buildings, the streets, the vehicles moving, the people moving, the ships in the harbor, the airport, the airplanes coming in and out. There was tremendous activity, and practically everything I saw really emanated from economic life. It all emanated from economic life. Even on the people, it was mostly the clothes that I saw moving along, just a little bit of the person. But mostly the clothes one saw going along. The cars, the buildings, the ships, all that, apart from nature itself, of course, all that was an emanation of economic life. That's what one sees.

But then when I looked a bit further, I saw traffic lights coming on and off. I saw cars, always on one side of the road rather than on the other. I saw a certain orderliness in the buildings, in the ships and the way they moved, and the airlines, the way they moved. They didn't crash into each other. So I began to see a certain ordering that came into life, into this human activity. People are allowed to build here and not build there. A certain protection you could see. People could walk the streets. They were free to walk the streets, and there were policemen there to protect and make certain the laws were fulfilled. One could look further into the buildings, and then there was a building that related actually to lawyers, solicitors and contracts for this whole realm. One could see just beyond the physical realm of bringing things into order.

Then beyond that, much more difficult to directly perceive, you could say, was something else. What went on in many of these buildings? What were the schools? What were the ideas that had created all this? What was this culture? What brought these particular types of buildings, what brought the architecture to the buildings? What were the thoughts that created the motor cars? When you saw a motor car going along, what was the thought that created it? When the light turned from green to red, the light itself is a result of economic life, and what the red spoke and what the green spoke touched the rights life. But the thoughts that had gone in, the technology that had gone into producing that red light and green light emanated from cultural life.

So here in the city one saw all things, but almost in different layers. If you go through the streets and you observe, you can begin to see these things. If one takes a little time and one learns to ask the question: What is one looking at?

In each of these three spheres, what is important is that they find their own center, their own direction. The whole of our cultural life should find its own direction and not be controlled by the state or economic life. At the moment, economic life is extremely dominant and tends to control much of our cultural life. To a certain extent, it controls the state. It controls the forming of laws. *But these three spheres must be separated.* Economic life has to find its own ordering, and the realm of state, the realm of the rights, that sphere of human activity where everybody's opinion is of equal value, must find its own center. Our cultural life must be free and must find its own center.

If you look at the human being, the threefold nature, first you'll find the nervous system. The brain and the nervous system have their center in the head. It has its own laws. It functions out of its own laws. If one looks at the rhythmic system—circulation of the blood, the breathing—there you get another system which works out of entirely different rules, entirely different laws, and it has a center, so to speak, in the heart and lungs. It works in quite a different way. The lymph system and the metabolic system are an entirely different system, working, again, according to different laws. What very often is good for the metabolic system can be poisonous for the nervous system, and yet the human being is one. You'll never find a nervous system going along by itself. In the social life, too, we've got to find these three.

Now we can look at it again slightly differently by looking at the polarities. If we look at this cultural life and we look at economic life, we find there an absolute polarity. I've touched on one aspect of it, but here we have polarities, opposites. In cultural life, we really demand freedom. It's necessary that individual human beings are free to be themselves, are not controlled in their thinking, in their creativity, by others. But if you think of economic life, can you be free in economic life? Can you be free not to eat? Can you be free to eat off a plate and not leave a dirty plate that needs washing up? Are you free to wear clothes that never get dirty, that don't have to be laundered? Are you free to transfer your thoughts from here to my wife in England without a telephone? You are not free. In economic life, we are not free. We cannot walk across the floor without actually wearing our shoes out and soiling the floor. Every time we walk through the world, we leave damage behind us. We are unfree and so we have to clear each other's mess up, if I can put it that way. We help each other. In cultural life, we have to arrive at freedom. In economic life, we're not free.

In cultural life, we create that which arises out of our own individuality. If I can put it this way: Go to a concert where there's a choir singing—a big choir. There's an orchestra and a choir and you sit there and listen to the beautiful music with these people singing, and then you ask yourself the question. One always has to do this in the actual place. We can sit around here and talk about social questions, but you never really understand until you go out in the world and ask these questions. There you ask yourself the question: Why are they singing? And even if you focus on a particular singer—and then to yourself say, why are they singing?—You'll come inevitably to the answer that they're singing because they need to sing. They need to sing out of their very being. And this, of course, is a particularly good example because these choruses are not paid. They nearly always do it voluntarily because they need to sing. I know one, the chairman of the Anthroposophical Society in England, used to sing in a choir, and he confirmed this absolutely. People sing there because they need to sing, and they actually need an audience. Really, they should pay us to listen to them. It's true of the orchestra and others. (It actually becomes distorted slightly; when one is paid to create, a certain distortion comes in.) In the first place, the teacher, the artist, the scientist, does it because he needs to out of his own inner being. Cultural life in the first place arises out of egoism.

In economic life, we have to arise to the polarity, to altruism, to brotherhood. No individual can actually create for himself. It all goes out to the others. So here again we get a polarity. In cultural life we have to become fully awake. Living in this consciousness soul area, we really rise as far as possible to being awake. If we want to think, if we want to understand, if we want to know something, we've got to be completely awake to it.

But if you look at economic life, there you will find is a certain condition of being asleep. And it's very interesting, when you follow people in business, industry, people in finance: How do they arrive at their decisions—to develop the industry in this direction or that, to manufacture this or that? Is there a market for this? If I bring this into the market, will it sell well or not? You'll nearly always find that those people who develop big industries, big businesses, work out of a sense for the market. They work out of their senses—they sense it; they don't think it through. You find this very strongly, for instance, in the financial market. In the stock exchange in London I often watch the financial futures market where they're buying and selling. They have to make decisions within seconds. When something is for sale, something happens over there: Do I buy the stock at this price? Is it going to go up? Is it going to go down? These are very often young people, and because it's very intense, they exhaust themselves quickly. They're not necessarily university graduates. They're not people who are terribly bright. They might be, that's not against them, but they're people who can make quick decisions, who develop a sense for the market, a sense for the movement of prices, and so forth.

Again, if you read many of the actual business journals, the financial journals, you often find a sense of play, a certain type of humor that is play, almost of a childish quality, as though things are not really worth a lot. Economic life has a certain relationship to the future. We are not yet awake in economic life; there's always a potential relationship to the future. In our whole cultural life, we're really relating, you could say, to the super-sensible nature, to that which in us touches the super-sensible nature, and in economic life, that which is of the sensible, which we can see or touch with our ordinary senses. In cultural life, we reach beyond the senses, the ordinary senses to the "super" senses.

If I took a blackboard, I could look at the economic life that produced the blackboard and the chalk. I could continue that economic activity by putting the chalk onto the blackboard, by just lines or whatever, or I could do that in a quite different way, by actually writing something on it. What I write, the chalk on the blackboard, is a continuation of economic life, but that which shines through what I've written, the words which are not in the chalk itself, but shine through (just as you read a book, 26 letters, and you see the same letters over and over and over again and yet you read something entirely different), that which shines through them is cultural life, and that's the point where these two meet.

Now another aspect. If we go back in history, we come to a time before Egypt and ancient civilizations when you could say the whole of social life was guided, was ruled, by the divine commandments through the wisdom of the priesthood, through the prophets, by the divine oracle. The whole of social life—what laws were formed, even as to when one went to war, when one planned the crops, how one worked with the metals—all this came through the priesthood, through the divine ordering of things. They were the theocracies, in which everything came through the divine ordering of things.

There are remnants of that left. But as humanity evolved, as this evolution developed in the divine ordering of things, the gods receded. A veil came down between the divine world and the human being, and we could no longer see the divine. This ordering, the divine ordering, disappeared, and what was the divine commandments was replaced by the law, man-made law, the realm of the state. When we could no longer live by the ordering of God, something had to replace it. When we no longer take divine commandment as important or as something that orders our lives, then unless we create our own law, what have is Chaos. So humanity had to create something to replace divine commandment. It's extremely inadequate, and we see that in the constant conflict between the law and conscience. It's a problem of our time—this conflict between conscience and law. This realm of our state, of law that we live by today, replaced the old divine commandment. Here you get something which was touched on in the Bible when Christ said,"Render unto Caesar the things of Caesar's and unto God the things that are God's." To differentiate between the realm of the state and the realm of the divine—how do we differentiate that?

In the future, we will begin to awaken to a perception of the other being—the divine in the other human being. Rudolf Steiner brings this lovely picture: If you take something like the Pacific Ocean, and if you take a glass, a beaker, and you take a little of the water of the Pacific Ocean, you can't say, "In this glass, I have the Pacific Ocean." But you do have something of the Pacific Ocean in that glass. You have something of the substance of the ocean. And so you can't say in another human being, there is the divine, just as in the glass, you can't say there is the Pacific Ocean. But in every human being, there's something of the substance of the divine, and there every human being is equal. In the realm of the states, in the realm of the law, we arrive at equality; and in the perception of the other human being, in that which, so to speak, is of the nature of the divine, of the substance of the divine, there also is an equality. When we can awaken to that, when humanity evolves slowly in the future to the point when that becomes a reality, then the realm of the law, the realm of the state, will no longer be needed because we will not harm that other person. We will not steal from him. We will bring in an ordering out of that recognition. But now, this will be arrived at not by ordering from without, but from within the human being. So here also we have a polarity.

That's really what I wanted to bring today. I hope I've given you a little bit of a picture—probably many questions—but as you go through the streets, as you go through life, one can begin to observe these things at work. Begin to observe these spheres. You never get something entirely by itself. In ancient times, a human being was born into a situation. The human being was born into a family, into a tribe, into a people, into a class, into a work, into a place in society. You get remnants of this in the old caste system, still in India. You get it, I know, in one of the recent prayer books in the Church of England, where in the prayer you ask God to make you satisfied with that place in life into which God has put you.

But now the human being stands free. The human being stands in each sphere. The human being is not born to be a soldier, or born into the priestly caste, or born to be a peasant. Each human being is born individual and free. But when we look at him and we say: shopkeeper, policeman, teacher, we are actually taking away his freedom; we are putting a clamp on him. But if we look at him and see an individual human being, an individual spiritual being, who in this life is fulfilling the role of being a shopkeeper, a policeman, a teacher, then we're looking more truly.

Brotherhood in the School Community

Michael Spence

Good morning. I'd like to start this morning by saying a little bit about myself and that from which I'm speaking. I've worked at Emerson College for 23 years as the bursar, and a great deal of what I will be saying today will come out of my experience there. Emerson College is, of course, a college of adult education. It's rather different from a school; it has different kinds of problems. For instance, 85% of our students come from abroad, only 15% from England. They come from all over the world! We have them from Ghana; we have Zulus from South Africa; we have about 7 from Yugoslavia; we've got one from Hungary, from Russia, some from India, Pakistan. All these people have immense financial problems, so we have big financial problems, but of a different nature than Waldorf schools. We don't have parents. That, actually, is also a disadvantage. But it doesn't mean I can't address, directly, the sorts of problems that many of you are dealing with. This fact is important— it means you cannot copy us. If I bring a solution that we've arrived at, you cannot copy us. You've got to think it out for yourself, which actually is very healthy. That out of which we work is common to all of us. The actual solutions we find in one institution or another are for those institutions. So it's quite good that you will actually have to work. I hope out of my experience I can say something on which you can build. But, of course, I will be speaking from examples, and I shall be talking a great deal about Emerson College—not because I think it's the best place in the world, but because that's my experience. It is that out of which I speak.

Now, another thing. At the last conference in New Hampshire, there was a man who had been invited to the school to talk a week or two before the conference and he was still there and attended it. He was Werner Spalinger from the Zurich Waldorf School in Switzerland. I was very interested that he was there. I was very encouraged because that school has been going 60-62 years, and he has been at that school for 36 years. He confirmed nearly everything I said, out of his experience. That school is actually working with these ideas and Emerson has been actually working with these ideas, so, when I speak, I'm speaking out of 23 years experience dealing with the money at Emerson College. Perhaps I could just say that at Emerson College, of those 23 years, I think in 20 or 21 of them, we've actually made a surplus on the operating accounts. I just wanted to say this because some of the ideas I am going to present might sound strange, but don't say they don't work.

Now, what is a school? In a school, how does one look on a child? How does the teacher meet the child? What is it in Waldorf education that encourages the parents to send their children there? In the first place the teacher recognizes in the child a super-sensible nature, a spiritual being that has been born, that's come into this earth condition through birth, that existed pre-birth, that comes from the spiritual world. It always reminds me of that poem by Wordsworth, "Intimations of Immortality in Early Childhood," and that beautiful line about the young child that says they come "trailing clouds of glory from God Who is our Father." That's a beautiful picture of the child coming from pre-birth and bringing something with him. In the school, in the teaching, one fully recognizes the spiritual world out of which that child has come.

That's the basis of the whole education, and without that the whole of the education falls down. And yet, do we take that thought of the reality of the spiritual world right through the school into the dealings with the money? In fact, in nearly all our schools, that thought is cut off before it reaches the accounts. How can we take finances as an actual reality? The spiritual world is there as a reality. If that child, that being, comes out of the spiritual world and into the school, then isn't that spiritual world also a reality for the running of the school, the administration, the money? How do we begin to work with the money in the school taking full account of the reality of the spiritual world? That, I think, is the question we have to face today.

On the basis of these ideas, we come to the way we work in dealing with, for example, salaries on a needs basis. More and more people in the world at large are beginning to work in this way, with some very interesting ideas in many different places. If we're not careful, the anthroposophical institutions are actually going to be left behind. They're going to be left in the dark and then they'll fail. The world is moving on, and we're still stuck sometimes 60-70 years ago. I put this as a challenge to you.

Let's look at the finances. Of course, it would be good to have much more time, a week or even more to really look at the whole of economic life, because the real economy is, as I said yesterday, the actual things we use—the buildings, the materials, et cetera—and the money only enables us, so to speak, to reach these. When we're paid salary, it's in order that the teachers, the members of staff, can buy their food, buy their shoes, buy their clothes, and so forth. The clothes are the consequence of economic life, but we've got to skip that part and come directly to the money because that's really what the school uses. The school is not an economic institution, it's a cultural institution.

Now I'd like to look particularly at salaries and at fees to give you more of a sense of the way we work, and I think the direction that more and more people are beginning to work. What is a salary? What is a wage? (When I talk, I will usually use the term "staff" because at Emerson College, we treat all members of staff, whether they're teaching staff, maintenance staff, catering staff, office staff—the same. So I shall use the term "staff" because I am used to it and that, I think, is the right way to approach this particular problem.)

What is a salary? Is it a purchase of labor? Is teaching a purchase? An actual exchange? If one looks historically at this salary, whether it's a salary or a wage, one can look at it in different ways. But if you go back say to Greek times and you look at the Greek culture, you can ask: What was the culture economically based on? It was based on slavery. Without slavery, the Greek culture could not have existed. It was grounded on an economic base in slavery. And what was the slave? The slave was a human being who was owned entirely by another human being. If you owned a slave, you had absolute right over that slave—the rights of life and death—the whole human being was owned. And then, if you follow this history up into the Middle Ages in Europe, there you see that slavery disappeared; but something remained which was still a remnant of it. That remnant was the various forms of serfdom. In serfdom, the whole human being is not owned, but part of the human being is still owned. Another human being has absolute right over a part of a human being. There's a certain ownership there.

There is a story that's very important to me, a biography of a man by the name of Lord Shaftsbury, who lived in England during the last century. With the title of Lord, he, of course, came from the land-owning aristocracy, and he owned large areas of land in the south of England. So here was a man who was born into the aristocracy who had his position in life through birth. He was a very fine man. He struggled immensely in order to overcome poverty—to help the children, for instance, in the streets of London who had nowhere to go, no school, many of them no home. He formed schools in London, and he struggled with the mill owners of the north, because there children and women were having to work through the night, very often in appalling conditions for long, long hours, six days a week. Many of these young children became deformed because of the appalling conditions. He tried to bring about a law which restricted the number of hours people were allowed to employ children. He tried to bring it to a maximum of ten hours a day. No one was allowed to be employed for more than ten hours a day. It's very interesting: The mill owners listened to his particular philosophy because he firmly believed that he was born out of a divine guidance as, so to speak, a leader. He owned the land, and that was part of the divine ordering of things. His peasants, his farm workers could never reach his height, and that too was part of the divine ordering. They were born to serve him and he was responsible for their soul life; he made certain there was a church there and a school for their children. He cared for them, but they had their place.

The mill owners of the north said, "The human being is free. I'm not responsible for your soul life; you can come and work for me if you want, or you needn't. If you come to work for me, I will pay for your hours. But you needn't." The fact that they'd probably starve if they didn't was probably a little bit forgotten. But there they said the human being was free. They could become mill owners too if they worked hard enough. There was nothing stopping them, and many of them worked their way up. It's very interesting, this balance. Lord Shaftsbury, in a certain sense, belonged to the past, and the mill owners in a certain sense, belonged to the future. But here you see a remnant of the old slavery; the individual had to sell his work to the mill owner. The wages he received, the time he had to work in the mills, was still a remnant of the old slavery. When we pay people, when we purchase their labor, when we still think in terms of purchasing a person's labor, when we still talk about the labor market, we're still thinking in these terms and treating people in that ancient way, which is a remnant of the old slavery.

Now, in our time, humanity has taken that step finally to free the human being. That, certainly in England, and I think elsewhere, is what a lot of our industrial unrest, industrial strikes, are about—the demand of the individual finally to be free. And that will become a greater and greater demand.

Some years ago there was a particular strike in England, in an engineering firm. Their employees went on strike, demanding a ridiculously high wage increase, something like 35% when inflation at that time was about 8%. It was quite ridiculous. It was quite clear if this demand were met, the firm would go bankrupt. A newspaper reporter talked to one of the trade union leaders and put this to him: "If your demand is met, your employers will all go bankrupt. Your employees will lose their jobs." The reply of this trade union leader was remarkably interesting and if one observes and reads the papers, one finds this sort of thing time and time again. The reply went something like this: "Yes, we know if our demand is met, our firm will go bankrupt." They recognized that. But he went on to say, "But so long as our wages are calculated on the same basis of the other inputs to the factory, then we have to strike."

This is a remarkable statement: "Then we have to strike." It is as though they experienced in themselves something they couldn't control. So long as their wages were still calculated as other inputs, as other materials, then they sensed an evolutionary power in the depths of their souls—that they had to strike.

When reasonable people act unreasonably, then one has to look for a deeper cause. We need to read into the signs of what's going on around us. We see these evolutionary forces and when we touch on wages, when we pay people for their labor, whether it's a teacher or an engineer or electrician, we're touching something that touches the depths of their souls and belongs to the past and does not belong to today. We have to break this old thinking, and this is a big question.

How do we begin to pay people today? It is not paying, it is not a purchase of their labor. I often have this question: If one had arrived in the Greek times as an economist and said, "It is wrong to purchase a slave. Slavery is not right. One has to find a different way of paying people other than slavery," they would have said that the whole of culture would collapse because no one would ever work. I think the same question is before us today. As the Greek might well have found it impossible to imagine the free market, a culture based on a free society, can we imagine a culture based on a quite different way of paying people? So how in our own institutions do we begin to deal with salaries? Can we begin to get away from the concept of purchase?

Perhaps I can put it another, quite different way: If I earn my livelihood as a lecturer, I have certain needs. I need to live, I need clothes, and so forth. I need some money. Now, who should pay for my needs? You see, if I'm giving a lecture, say to 40 people, and one more comes into that room, it doesn't make any difference to my lecture. But if I have a plate of cakes, there are 20 cakes on a dish, and one of you comes and wants a cake, you pay me for that cake. You take a cake. Now there are 19 left and someone else comes, gives me something and there's an actual exchange, and now there are 18 left. And eventually there's one left, and then there's none left, and for the next person there's nothing at all. This is economic life.

But when one talks in cultural life, say of something like a lecture, suppose that I'm giving a lecture to 5 people, it's not easy to give a lecture to 5 people. You usually end up giving a poor lecture. If one more person comes in the door, do the 5 get less of the lecture because now there are 6? Actually it could become a better lecture. So you see, we've got to think in an entirely different way. You cannot think in terms of ordinary economics. You have to arrive at it quite differently. One could say logically that the first person would pay the total full fee and all the others pay nothing. This doesn't quite make sense either, so we have to arrive at a different basis.

At Emerson College, when the student pays a fee, we look at it as a contracted contribution. It's not a free gift. Some people use the term free gift, but I find that is not true, because if they don't make that free gift, I'm going to chase them out. There is a contradiction. It's a contracted contribution. I have, as a teacher, certain needs, and those people who come to benefit from that contract to meet a certain portion of my needs. And the college contracts to run certain classes, to be there, to continue it through the year, to have these classes. The student contracts to meet a certain portion of our needs. Then the question is:

How does one arrive at this contract, this fee? I will come back to this question in a few minutes. First I'd like to look a bit more at the salaries.

With salary we talk about needs. Now here one is touching, one is bridging what I'll be talking about later—this whole rights life and economic life. You see, the way we arrive at salaries, the way we decide to deal with our salaries, that really belongs to rights life. How we do it—whether we as a group decide to do it on a needs basis or some scale of this type or that type—really arises out of the community. How do we want to work? But how much the individual gets within that scale, how much the individual gets within that framework—that really is a matter for the individual, it touches economic life.

So here's a point where these two spheres meet and each has its own area to influence. How does one arrive at individual needs? What are individual needs? That, of course, is a very difficult question. Imagine yourself coming to work at Emerson College and it's agreed that you'll come to teach or whatever. In the first place your new colleagues will have to meet you to decide if you are the right person. Then there comes the point of asking, "Can we meet your needs?" The picture here is: If we recognize you're coming to, say, teach painting at Emerson College, first of all, the other art teachers have to recognize what you are going to bring out of your own capacities, out of your own destiny. Is the connection you have with color, painting, with your work, really what they want at the college? Will you complete the circle of colleagues, complete the work? Is that what the students want to come to meet? That is the first question, you could say, which belongs to the cultural-spiritual life. Has your destiny brought you here? That has to be recognized by the other teachers, particularly the teachers involved in art. I, as an administrator, can't judge that. It has to come from somewhere else.

Then we have to find out whether you as an individual are welcomed into this circle. That question is then brought to the staff meeting, that we're thinking of inviting so and so to teach painting here. Everybody in that circle of colleagues, in the community, has an opportunity to welcome that person or say I have difficulty working with that person, and I don't think he should be working here because it's going to create a problem. So here we touch the rights life. This procedure is so that we can all take that into our consciousness.

Then there's the question of the salary. At Emerson the picture is, if that person is the right person to come and teach here, he can only do that if he is freed from having to make his own shoes, grow his own cabbages. He must be freed from having to get a job to earn money. So we have to free him. So we say to him,"What are your needs? What do you need in order to be free so that you can work with our students?" Now imagine if I put that question to you. You have to think what your needs are. It's a very difficult question, and time and time again, I come to get the answer back, "Well, what is the average, what do you pay other people?"

This is a very real question, because a person wants to know what is the community that he's coming in to. What is the recognized standard of living? Is it very low? Is it high? What is the standard of living? Instinctively a person wants to adjust to that. Often people can't come to a definite figure, so very often I will suggest a figure. I know roughly their situations, and we might go through certain figures, and sometimes I'll suggest a figure. I make it quite plain that they can come at any time, and I would expect them to come, say, in six months time to say how it's working out—whether it's too little or too much, and to help them really to enter into this commonly accepted standard of living.

It's very interesting, you sometimes get a person who comes from a wealthy area. We had one member of staff who'd been in Dornach, Switzerland, for a long time. He, himself, wasn't Swiss. In fact, he was American, but he had lived there some time and so he was used to a fairly high standard of living in a community that had a high standard of living. And he came to Emerson College. He took two years to adjust. He slowly came down and down, quite out of his own will, out of his own recognition, and actually, he went way down below everybody else and then remained there. Very interesting to watch. And so very often one has to give a person time to adjust into his new living situation. We have to help them. And then once a year, we have a meeting. Individuals, members can come at any time and say this has happened, that has happened, I need some money for this or that. And it's basically their decision. They don't come and ask, "Can I have?" Some very often do, but that's not really what we expect. It should be much more: "This is my need," a fully recognized fact. This is my need—try to arrive at it objectively—I need an extra £200. Then we might talk about it, but basically, it's your decision and I pay it.

We do have a committee that sometimes discusses this. If a person's demand is high, we might question it. Once a year, we have a meeting and we discuss salaries, we discuss the finances. To that meeting we bring a number of things. One is, and I constantly reiterate this, that it is not Emerson College that pays your salary. It's your students who pay your salaries. Your students. And every time you ask for money, an increase, you are putting the fees up of your students. I remember bringing certain figures once—I happened to work it out that particular time—that if we all asked for an increase of £100, the fees would go up £40. So the teachers, the staff, know that they are raising the fees of their students, and if they ask too much, then students will not be able to come.

I really try to bring this home, this picture, that the college, or myself as the administrator of finance, is purely a mediator between these two. Purely the fulcrum that keeps the two in balance. This really has to be conscious in the staff. Now there are certain things that help there. We try to work at things as colleagues and we manage to avoid, to a large extent, this whole sense that one is an employee. One just has to work and work at it.

At the college I can't say it works 100% all the time. We have many problems; many individuals, of course, have problems with these ideas.

I have sometimes someone who's been there 15 years who still comes to bring me a question, and I know it's out of the "purchase-of-labor" thinking that still exists. This are deeply ingrained in us. It's ingrained in our education. We are exposed to these ideas from birth. How often does a mother say to a child, "Don't waste that, it costs money"? You're sowing a seed.

Every year we have this meeting and out of that meeting, we then bring back what we need. Sometimes we suggest a figure for inflation, and we say if you don't give any figure, then we'll increase your salaries by this inflation figure. Or this year we said, things are rather tight, so we are delaying this whole procedure six months; this was discussed and agreed, so nobody had any increase for six months, and then we brought these figures and we said, if you don't say anything, you'll be paid the same as before, so no increase. But if you want an increase, you've got to say what increase you need—so many pounds or a percentage, or whatever. Quite a number of people said that they could manage without. So that is the way we deal with salaries.

To me, one cannot really successfully deal with the needs-based salary system, and I don't suggest that anyone rush home suddenly and say they intend to have a needs-based salary system. It creates immense problems. It's much easier if you come, I don't have to look you in the face and discuss it with you, but I look at a figure here and say, "Well, one wife, two children, so many years' experience, that's so much and that's what you get." It solves a lot of problems. To have no such scale, you have to meet the individual every time and talk it over. Every time there's a question, you meet that individual and talk it over. It makes life much more difficult. You meet the human being face to face, over and over. One can really do this, I think, only if one really accepts the reality of karma and destiny. If one doesn't accept the reality of karma and destiny, then it's extremely difficult to work on a needs basis.

Now at the college, because our students can't afford very much, when new members of staff come to join us, we have to tell them what they're coming into. They're coming into a place which is financed 90–

95% out of the fees of the students. We have no endowments, no big money coming from elsewhere. We're funded in our current account by the fees that come from the students to about 90–95%. So they're coming into this particular situation. We cannot afford to pay them a high salary. We cannot afford to pay them the salary which enables them to buy their own houses and put money aside for their retirement. They have to face their own future. They have to recognize that in coming to work at the college, they're not going to have that security into the future which many people demand today. That must be their decision. Do they really want to come?

I remember one young man who joined us many years ago. He had a family, two children, and at that particular time, we were just not in a position to buy a house for him, or even find a house for him. And yet, it was important that he come to work at the college. Circumstance brought him at a particular time, a time when we couldn't find a house for him. His father was prepared to put up quite a lot of money for a substantial deposit on a house, but he would need a mortgage as well. So for that particular person, we had to agree that we'd pay him enough to buy his own house on mortgage.

So you see, if one feels that everybody is the same and we talk about fairness and everybody should be the same, then that becomes unfair. It becomes unfair to the rest of us who will end up with no house. But if one recognizes karma and recognizes that people have different paths, different destinies, and here was an individual who was brought to the college at a particular time, a time when it was not possible to buy in a house, and one recognizes that perhaps that's in his destiny, it's in his karma to have to deal with the problems of house ownership. If that's a reality, then one can accept it. Then one can accept for one person one thing and for another person something else. But one must recognize this. If one doesn't face these realities, then there can be problems.

One other thing I think is necessary. I remember someone said to me once: We live in the Michaelic Age, the age of the rulership of the archangel Michael. One of the problems of this Michaelic Age is to develop the courage to face the future that we have prepared for ourselves. This is a tremendous picture. But before birth we, so to speak, look into our future life and we set ourselves certain tasks. We develop certain strengths for certain tasks that we have to face, and very often these tasks are problems, or disasters, or difficulties we have to get through. We need to develop strength through solving that difficulty for going through that difficulty in the future. So if one can live with that thought, then when a difficulty comes in the future—if I find on my retirement that the college has gone bankrupt, and I have immense problems—that is a problem that I have placed there for myself and I have got the courage to face it.

It's not easy to always work in this way. But that is the way we try, and we have a great advantage that there's no one working at the college who is not in one way or another connected with anthroposophy. A person might not be a member of the Anthroposophical Society but still work out of, you could say, the substance of anthroposophy.

When we look at fees, that again is not a purchase. As I say, it's a contribution. Now, most of our students come for only one year, some for two, a few for three or four years. So with the majority who come for one year, we cannot work in the way we'd like to work. We'd love to work also that the students contribute according to their abilities. However, students are really only able to develop the thoughts to do that after they've been with us at least a year or two. But a student who applies—has perhaps just met anthroposophy, inspired by something, and feels he wants to come because he is an artist—has just his ordinary everyday thoughts, and he hasn't yet got the thoughts with which to deal with these sorts of questions. So we have to have a fee.

We arrive at the fee in the following way. Suppose it takes £10,000 to run the college—it actually takes a lot more—but just take that figure. It takes £10,000 to run the college, pay the salaries, and suppose we have 100 students. They would each have to pay £100. Now, if we had fewer students, our cost is still £10,000 because we run the same number of courses; we have 9 different courses. So with a few students less, our costs are basically the same, with very little difference. Now suppose there aren't 100 students; there are only 80. They would each have to pay £125. But then another 10 students come who can pay, say, £80 each. If they pay £80 each, the original 80 students won't have to pay £125; they would have to pay only £115 because now there's this extra lot. There might be another 10 people who can pay £40 each, which means the 80 won't pay £115, they'll pay £110 each. You see, the people who have less subsidize the people who pay more.

No one has ever disputed that. Because in a certain sense, it's true. Because we take people paying less, we can reduce the higher figures for everyone else. Then some scholarship money comes in, which means that £110 can be brought down to £105, and that becomes what we announce as our fee. That allows us, you see, not to give scholarships; we don't have a pot of money, and if you can only afford £40, we take £60 out of it and put into our fee account. Rather we then contract with you that your contribution is £40, and this gives flexibility.

These figures are arrived at out of experience of the sort of proportions that people need. Now also I put to the students: We are a world college, and if you look around the world, people are born into entirely different situations. Some people are born into a situation where even £40 is almost an impossible amount. Others are born into a situation where frankly £105 is not very much. So as a world college, we ought to have something in our fee structure that begins to reflect it, that begins to reflect that they pay out of the situation in which they're born, so to speak, or live, rather than based on the situation into which they're coming. I always receive an immensely positive reaction from the students. I've never had anyone say, "I don't see why I should pay £105 in order that others can pay £40." I have had a few come and say, "Well, frankly, I think I ought to pay more than £105." I've never asked for that, but I find that some consider this when they are aware of the whole situation at the College.

The Life of Rights
in the School Community

Michael Spence

Some years ago, three young women turned up at Emerson College. Two were Brazilian and one was Spanish. They wanted to come to the college. When one talked to them and discovered the path that had led them to the college, talked about their life and the various events and meetings which had brought them to the college, one could find a certain ordering in this. It was not haphazard; it was not coincidence. Time and time again one observes a very interesting story of how one event leads to another event in a person's life, and he or she eventually is brought to Emerson College. So these two Brazilians, who had tried to found a school in Brazil and found that they didn't have the basis for beginning it, came to Europe and through certain circumstances met anthroposophy and Emerson College. In the meantime they met another Spanish girl, and they arrived together at the college with no money.

They were very fine young women, and one really experienced what brought these people here, to this college. They wanted to go back to Brazil to do real work. They came to prepare themselves to work with children. This was not coincidence; they were brought to the college because this was where they should come. One doesn't always have that experience, and one has to be very careful that it is a true experience. It's easy to say every lovely person ought to come to Emerson College and get caught up in that. So by observing carefully what was brought, I had a strong experience that these three had to be at the college.

I've had quite a number of these experiences over the years, and eventually I came to this question: If they've been brought to the college by their guardian angel, their destiny, the spiritual world—if this college is being created for these people, then should just a lack of money stop them? Surely there must be the money somewhere to enable them to come. If they are brought to the college in order to be at the college, then surely somewhere, somehow, it must be possible. If the spiritual world brings them, it must be possible. That to me has been a question for quite a long time now.

I am quite convinced that, one way or another, it must be possible for those people to come. It might be that they have certain connections, certain possibilities of raising the money which they haven't met yet. It might be that I have certain connections, or that Emerson College somehow has connections which could find the money for these three people. It could be that actually there will be enough other students paying full fees to cover our costs, so three extra people is not going to be a big burden on the college and we can carry them without fees, as long as they cover their board and lodging. One of the Brazilian girls had a husband, which was a certain asset, because he could get a job. There are all these possibilities.

This is my question: How can one begin to work this way because one is looking into the future? I am quite certain that, when those three come, a great deal of the future depends on my decision or the teachers' decision, because in this area I work with the teachers. The teachers must recognize that these three should be here. It's not really my task, but I still very often have that experience, and I always try and work with the teachers. So I get this experience sometimes that the spiritual world waits for the decision that we have to make. It waits for us to make the right decision, and the right decision could be that they should go away and come back another year. It's very difficult to know, but if we make the right decision, then I think something else can happen. It could be that there are one or two students wondering whether to come to the college this year or next year, and suddenly they are prompted to feel this is the year to come because they need to meet these people, and they have quite enough money, so we'll have enough students with fees.

You know, one gets lots of appeals nowadays. I'm sure you've experienced them, appeals through the post. Very often you look at them and chuck them into the waste paper basket because there are just too many of them. But occasionally one catches your eye and you suddenly have the feeling: I'd like to support that. What makes you feel you'd like to support that? What makes you suddenly see it?

There are many different ways to work, but how does one work this way in the future? To me, if one starts working with money, this is an essential part of it. It makes working with money one of the most interesting works there is, because it's so creative. It has this artistic quality, when one gets away from the numbers.

I'd like to bring a certain picture. It's a bit complex, but I'll try to make it clear. Rudolf Steiner talks about three areas of cognition. As one goes on the path of inner development, one reaches three stages of cognition: imagination, inspiration, and intuition. Steiner characterized them like this: If you stand before a picture—a picture by a great painter or a painter who's tried to reveal in his painting a certain truth of nature, a truth of mankind, a truth of the spiritual world—what you see is just canvas and pigments of color. Outwardly, physically that's what you see, just pigment. But what is revealed through them is that which the painter is trying to put into expression. By looking at it carefully through the pigments, you recognize this truth as it is revealed through the painting. That is akin to imagination.

But then one can take it a step further. If you stand before a canvas when the painter is in the process of bringing the painting about—he's just begun to paint the picture—then you have to reach much further to arrive at that truth which is coming into being, the truth which is being revealed. It's not there yet fully, but it's coming into being. So to reach that which is coming into being, one has to rise to inspiration.

Then, in the third, one can stand before the empty canvas, and there are the pigments, the paint brushes, et cetera. The painter is going to paint the picture but hasn't started it yet. Here one has to rise to a much higher level of cognition in order to reach that which will come about, which hasn't even begun yet, but which will come about. How can one reach that which will come about?

Rudolf Steiner likens these three stages to three areas in economic life: to commodity, labor, and capital. Capital he places alongside intuition, the blank canvas. Now let us look at the cultural institution and education (education, of course, stands in the cultural life). It would take me rather a long time to explain the various circulation of money—how one rises from three types of money, from purchase money, loan, and gift—which arises out of capital. But the gift is the final area in which capital as capital disappears.

I find this a very interesting picture. In dealing with the money in a school, one is dealing with money which is on the level not of the everyday money, or purchase money, not on the level of loan, which really is what industry bases itself on, but on the level of money when capital finally finds its fulfillment and disappears as gift; this is upon what cultural life depends. That is akin you could say, to the blank canvas, with which you have to rise to the level of intuition to know what will come about—not what has happened, not what you can count, not what you can budget for, but what you can really picture will come about. You stand before the young child. How do you know what will come about? So when those students come and stand before me or sit before me and ask to come to the college but they haven't enough money, how does one then come to a decision of what will come about, what will lie in their destiny, what will be achieved, and what may come forth? It's a very difficult question, and now I'll consider it from another point of view.

Let's consider it from the point of view of the teacher. Let's say you need a new teacher, in our case perhaps to teach painting. A fine person comes and wants to join the college, and we feel he belongs here, but he's got a large family. We had one recently, a man, who had five children and, of course, a wife. With all those children, the school fees at Michael Hall for his children would be high. He'd need a large house; he'd need a car; it would be a very heavy bill on the college. Then one has to decide: Do we need this? If we just look at the budget, if we just look at how much money we have, the answer must be no. Then one has to ask the question: What is the future? I ask this question quite seriously: If that person is a teacher, for instance, are the young people who are looking for him out there?

Of course, I'm looking at it in the context of Emerson College, and you have to find the way that you look at this in the context of your own school. It's not the same. But out of your experience, out of your observation of how things work, you have to learn to observe: If you do something here, what happens later on? Learn to observe this. And so, if we are to take this person on, are there people out there who are waiting to come to Emerson College, but they are waiting for this particular teacher to be there? If they are waiting for this teacher to be there, and if we accept this teacher, we actually have an increase in students, but we will never know until they are there.

It's easy to get a bit Luciferic about this and believe everything will work out right. It doesn't always. These are difficult decisions, but you will not know the answer until you have made a decision one way or the other.

I remember on several occasions when the enrollment for a particular course, for instance, was declining, and things were going a bit difficult, and then we made a change, perhaps a new person came. One particular occasion I remember very particularly: We took on a new member of staff. On other occasions we made other changes which were fairly costly. There was a lot of discussion whether we should do them because they were expensive, but we made the changes. Immediately there was an increase in students. I've seen this on several occasions. On at least two of these occasions, and I think on a third, it was not possible for all these people to have known that a change had been made. It was not possible for them to know, nor did it take a year for the increase to happen (time for the word to get around). The increase was immediate. These are observations. So one questions: Was that a right decision we made? Perhaps it was a bit costly, but people were waiting for it.

This is an area in which a great deal more research needs to be done. We need to work in this way. We need to learn to observe—with patience and a certain courage—if destiny is really working here. You never know, but you've got to make the decision, because until you've made that decision, nothing will happen. Today the gods won't indicate the correctness of a decision to you; that belonged to the past. To me, this is an extraordinarily interesting and important area of working with money; it's the most important. If we are to be truly Waldorf schools and anthroposophical institutions really working with the spirit, with destiny, then it must work right down into the money.

Now I'd like to go a little bit further and begin to move into the sphere of rights on a broader basis. Perhaps I can begin with another picture. A little while ago I was driving along with my wife and I came to a major road. To the left there was a bit of a brow coming down, and of course, driving on the correct side of the road in England one looks first left to see if someone is coming. Nothing was coming so I looked to the right; nothing coming. Then normally I would look to the left again. It is very interesting looking back on the event. I was quite conscience of the fact that something said to me, "You've already looked left, you needn't look again." I was quite conscious of that fact afterwards. So I pulled out and there was a car coming. It was a rather nasty accident. Both our cars were badly damaged. We were a bit shaken up and so was the other party.

Occasionally one has that moment of consciousness, a certain moment of grace, and I remember feeling that this was an experience brought about for some reason or other and I must be aware of everything that happens. I must learn from this experience. I must be fully conscience and not get caught up in the emotions and all the rest of it, but really be awakened to this moment. It's come about because the little voice told me not to look. Within minutes an Automobile Association man arrived, the other party asked the AA man to call the police, and within five minutes a policeman was there, actually two policemen. But I remember one particular one who was in charge. This was a very interesting situation. Here were two men, both in uniform. One had the policeman's uniform and he represented the law. The other had the uniform of the AA, and he really represented economic life, because he was going to repair our car, get it working, so that we could get back home.

I tried really to observe in this situation the difference between these two: two uniforms and two individualities who were wearing the uniforms. The policeman, afterwards, had a certain inquiry up at the college. He came to our house; he knew our address. My wife and he got talking. He had been in the Brighton bombing; he had been a policeman there. He had been a policeman in the coal-miners strike, and he talked about his experiences there, which he had found very, very unpleasant. I met him later on, and here was an individuality, a human being, whom actually I liked very much, but in the uniform, at the accident, he had to suppress his individuality. He had to be the law. I was conscious of this. At the time I felt in him that he was busting out to be human and say hello to me and treat me as a nice human being, but he couldn't. For I might have committed an offense, and he would have to give evidence, so he had to ignore my individuality. So I had to go along with that. He was fulfilling a role required by the law, required by society, a correct role, and yet he wanted to do something other in a certain sense.

The AA man was much freer, because he had come to help anyway. That was his task. But he also was an individuality, and to me this was a very strong experience of this separation, of the role one plays, the tasks one fulfills, and the individual human being who happens to be a policeman or who happens to be an AA man.

How can one take this division into our institutions, into our schools, into our colleges? How can we find that place where one meets as individuals rather than as teachers, as cooks, as parents? Where can we meet as individuals, as individual human beings, with everything that implies? Now, some of you might well have experienced or been involved in founding a new school or a new institution, as either teachers or parents, but particularly as teachers.

Very often you come to a certain experience. Two or three, perhaps four, of you come together and you feel you want to found a school. You haven't got much money. There might be one or two parents in your group who have a little money. Often this is what happens. So, you make a start. You scrape and stint, and you'll find that very often, if the thing is to be successful, there is a sort of unspoken opinion amongst the group. It is that you will live at a very low standard of living; you will give everything to this school.

There can be a common opinion, a sort of sense that you won't take holidays for this year, that you will contribute everything to the founding of this school. If you begin to become aware of this, you can become aware of a sense of a common standard of living that arises out of a sort of common opinion that might well be unspoken. It's very important, this feeling for a common standard or level of living and how this arises. It lives there amongst a certain group of people, and it arises out of the group of people, out of their intention to carry out their work, a work the purpose of which lies outside themselves.

This is a very important factor. If the purpose of such a work lies within yourself, it will founder. That is connected with the law that was read out at the beginning of this conference (Fundamental Social Law[2]). The purpose must be outside itself—with the children that need to come to this school, the children that are out there in the community as well as one's own, not just one's own. This sense of a common standard of living first of all can be very low, and as the school begins to develop, you will very often experience that this level, which arises out of common opinion, begins to rise. You can't go on indefinitely without a holiday. You can't go on indefinitely with the old shoes that have holes in them. Eventually you have to buy the new shoes for yourself, perhaps take a holiday. Again, very often unspoken, the sense of what is a reasonable standard of living begins to rise. Where does that common opinion find its source?

As the school develops, as it gets older, it has to become more conscious, and then one has to begin to take hold of it. It is my experience that Emerson College has gone through a life cycle much like a human being. In fact, the seventh year was like the seven-year-old child's change of teeth. This was, for the college, an extremely difficult year, not financially, but with the people. It was the beginning of the founding of many of the organs, the teachers meeting, and so forth. Then when we got to year 21, many of us had the extraordinary experience of suddenly finding ourselves standing alone. We had the real feeling that that which supported us, the spiritual beings which supported us, were withdrawing—like the parents who say, "Go stand on your own now. You are grown up. No longer must you rely on us." We began sensing that we had to make our own decisions. Several of us experienced this. So as the school develops, one has to take hold of these realities.

At the college we have what we call a staff meeting. Every week we have the faculty meeting. It's a meeting when all the teachers gather. The staff meeting, which also happens every week, is everybody who works at the college, irrespective of their position. Everybody who works at the college attends, and we meet every week. They all come, and in that meeting we very often start with a short study. It's a place of communication, what is happening, reports for instance. When I go back, I shall give the report of these conferences, of my journey here. They will be interested to hear what's happening in America. What are the tasks, what are the problems here? Are they different or are they the same? They will be interested, and I will give a report of that. And, for instance, if the council is dealing with a major question, it will come to that staff meeting, unless it's purely a teaching matter. Any more general questions—ideas for developing the college, the possibilities of new staff, changes—they all come to that staff meeting in the form of reports with time for discussion. Not for decisions—you can't make decisions among 50 or 60 people. So the members of the council, which is equivalent to your board hear the discussion. (At Emerson all members of council are members of staff; we have no parents or bodies outside so that is a difference.)

A member of staff who has an opinion knows it's heard by those people who make decisions. They are listened to. Now, in that staff meeting, one really meets as individuals who are carrying the work. That is, I think, one of the most important things is that people experience, and the experience must be reality, that in this circle I am recognized as a full human being carrying my share of the work of this totality and these are my colleagues. We refer to each other as colleagues. These are my colleagues—some teach, carrying the central work of the college; some work in the office, some work in the kitchen; some in the garden. We are all colleagues, each carrying our little bit of the work. That needs to live very strongly in the meeting as a reality.

Then there's something else in this meeting which one tries to keep alive, which one can experience. When perhaps the more wise teachers speak, when the leaders speak, who are leaders out of their capacity, very often one has an experience of light. One has an experience of light when people impart their knowledge, their understanding, their wisdom. Conversely, when someone else speaks who hasn't got that ability to speak, who is not a teacher but perhaps works in the garden, and yet out of his work has come to certain experiences of nature, experiences with people—if one listens properly, then one has an experience of warmth. One needs the two in any community. The one without the other is cold. That is an essential point of the college: the staff meeting in which we tried to keep these alive.

Also at Emerson College, because of our particular constitution, everyone who comes to work and stays for one or two years is invited to become a member of the Association. So, the college is owned by the people who work there, 90% of them. Again, it makes no difference what work you do; merely the fact that you work there, that it is your main work and you are basically working out of anthroposophy, are the important things.

I'd like to become a bit controversial. I have never worked at the college through a budget. I try to, so to speak, get the teachers involved in the work of the college, to arrive at decisions, not out of the money, but rather out of the "rightness" of the decision. We try to work out of that which the spiritual moment requires. How can one determine what is required out of the spiritual moment?

One has to use intuition. When we work in a school, we're dealing with money that belongs to the sphere of the cultural life. This money's value is not merely a pound for a pound, but it represents potential. It can become something which it isn't at present. We must work with finances in a cultural institution in quite a different way. We must think into the future about what could be, about the child or student or teacher who may be effected. If we don't work with money in this way, then the spiritual world will not be able to work with us.

The School as a Free Cultural Institution

Michael Spence

In conclusion, I'd like to start by looking at the question of the task of the administrator. By that I mean more than just the tasks of the administrator, but also the people involved in the administration of a school—What is their task, what is their role? There are many decisions that have to be made in a school, in a college—decisions about development, decisions about further work, decisions about the new teacher, decisions about policy. Really these decisions ought to arise out of that spirit that informs the whole—that spirit which lives in the school, which brings about or enables the very teaching to take place. This should live more consciously in the teaching body than anywhere else in the college. Those are the people, out of the nature of their work, out of the nature of their connections with the children, who should be the most informed, the most sensitive to the spirit that works in the whole. The decisions, the answers must find their origin in this group of individuals.

The decisions are formed; they rise out of the needs of the teaching, out of the purpose of the school. As an administrator (what you normally call here a business manager, we call a bursar in England), when I find my role, I don't see it really as a major decision maker. I have to be so sensitive and informed of the movement of money—I use that term—of the movement of money, and of what is happening. My task is really to bring that whole information, that whole understanding to the teaching body. I have a responsibility to make certain that the teachers take all these things into consideration, that they have the information, and that they make the decisions when they should.

I remember a particular incident at Emerson some time ago. There was a group that wanted to put up a new building. There was a big question in the college whether it should happen and whether they would get enough money. I remember for certain we put off the decision because there wasn't the money. People couldn't sense whether it should happen or not. I remember at a certain point several donations were made, and then it was felt that because these donations had been made, we could go ahead with the building. I found myself in quite a dilemma. I knew what really should come from my side; that is, the way the money had come. The money pointed in a direction that, perhaps, now is the time to build. But that was only half the picture.

I knew at that moment that if I brought that half picture, the decision would be made on it. The money would make the decision. That's what actually happened. This was in the council, which was mostly teachers, and in the council the other side was really not brought. I think they did not deeply enough perceive whether this particular impulse, out of the spiritual aspect, was ready. They left it to the money. At that point, there was enough money to begin and then the whole thing went wrong. The project has never been finished because no more money came. This, I think, is the task of the administrator: to try to enable the teachers to make the decisions they have to make. It's a partnership. The decision very often is between us. Someone comes to me, a teacher comes to me, and asks if we can afford a new whatever it is they need. I usually throw the question back at them and say, "Can we afford not to have it?" So this question must come in between, because I can usually find the money for one thing, but it means something else cannot happen. I try and give that question to these teachers.

Then there are the other questions which come. When you have a new institution, you go without things, and you have rooms without curtains. Then one day a teacher comes and says, "Look, I know where there's some cheap cloth, and one of our parents will sew it for me so we can have some curtains. It will cost only £20." I say to them, "No it won't. It will cost £100–£150, at least. Probably even more." I throw it back at them, because I know from my experience, and this is what I have to bring to them.

It might be necessary to make that decision, but they must know the movement. If they have the curtains and they get their curtains for £10, then what's the consequence? The next teacher needs curtains. You actually raise the standards in a certain part of the school, and that has consequences all around. You can take it further: nice new curtains and now the paint looks grotty, so let's paint the room. This all comes out of experience. I put that to the teacher. It will not cost £20; it will cost £150 or £200. Now, make your decision, because you have to decide whether those curtains are necessary. You have to teach in that room, so you must make the decision.

My task is to make certain that you know the facts and you know the consequences. That's how I see my task. Sometimes I do make the decision. I have an awful habit sometimes. Someone says, "I must have this. Can we have it?" And I'll say, "Well, I'll have to think about it." If they never come back to me, I know they didn't really need it, and often they don't. But, that's an aside.

There's another thing which is connected to that: Where does the guardianship of the spiritual impulse with regard to the teaching rest? That really rests quite obviously in the teachers, and most of them take this very seriously. They study, really study, to make themselves fit teachers, work at their own development, work at study, how to meet the child, how to be a good teacher. That rests quite consciously within the teachers. But where is the guardianship of the spiritual workings through the money? That rests on the administrator, I think. That really should rest on the administrator. So there is a real responsibility there that the parts become a whole.

Now, I'd like to look slightly further afield and take this more out into the wider scope, because I'd also like to ask the questions: What is one actually preparing the children for? What is one teaching the children? What is this world? What is going on in the world that one is preparing the children for? And is one preparing them? If we look in the world at large, what do we find? There are many different things one can see, but one thing I would like to bring is the domination of money, the absolute domination in a wide area of money.

Here is one symbol of that. If you go to one of the older cities, not probably in the U.S., but in Europe—the older cities in England or Wales and these various places, say, an interesting city, Ely—what do you see that stands central in such a city? It's a cathedral or the church. Ely is in a very flat part of England, around Norfolk, and in this flat which was one time covered by the sea, there's a hill. On the hill is the cathedral. You can travel for miles around and really imagine when that cathedral was built hundreds of years ago. What an inspiring sight for the whole community, that this cathedral stood tall there, and you imagine the people came up to that cathedral and saw the spire reaching up to the sky, the highest thing that the human being reached to. It must have been inspiring.

If you go into our big cities now, what has replaced the cathedral? What stands there tall? It is the banks and financial institutions. In the city of London, in the financial center is the National Westminster Bank, their head office. It's quite an inspiring building. It stands there tall, the tallest building in London at the moment. You can see it as you go to many different parts of London. Wherever there's a view, you can see that standing there. If you go up to it, you can look straight up at it because its a cantilevered building, so you can sort of stand right underneath it and look directly up. It's quite inspiring. This is our financial center. That to me is extremely symbolic. To go into a city (I remember doing it once in Detroit some years ago), one can stand in the city asking the question: What moves all this? It's the money that keeps everything in movement. It's the money.

How can we begin to control the money, because at the moment, the money controls us? To a very large extent, we are controlled by money. Our decisions are controlled by money. In our wider public life, how many decisions by government, by agencies, by individuals, and so forth, are controlled by the money? In our own institutions, when we quite objectively look in our own schools, how many decisions are made by the money? Much more than they should be, I do believe.

In the 1960s there was a very strong movement of many young people—particularly coming from here, from America—going to the East, to India. And what were they looking for? They were looking for brotherhood. They experienced, they had a sense that, really in this whole economic life, something was missing. There ought to be brotherhood and there was only freedom. There was only freedom, but they searched for brotherhood. They went, many of them, to India and such places, and there they found a form of brotherhood. Then they came back, and they tried to form cultural institutions based on brotherhood. They deserted the freedom, which was in economic life, went to the East, searched for brotherhood which they should have brought back to economic life, but they didn't. They brought it to the cultural life, but out of the very real search, out of the real longing for this.

Look at something like South Africa. I've watched the phenomenon of South Africa now for many, many years, some 25 years. I was in the Kenya Police during the Mau Mau uprising, so I have a certain experience of that sort of situation. I watched this phenomenon of South Africa and I found it extremely interesting that if one actually compares what's happening with South Africa in other parts of the world, one then is left with the question: Why does everybody get so worked up with South Africa and not with these other events in the world? Observe what's happening in Afghanistan, where millions of people were killed, women, children, families, farms, and still many are deeply suffering with maimed limbs. Yet we've almost forgotten about this, but about South Africa, people get worked up. I don't agree and I don't defend for one moment anything that's happening in South Africa. I'm interested in why people get worked up. I've seen it in young people's eyes, when you mention South Africa, there's a certain reaction. Then I ask the question: When such a thing happens, surely there's some deeper foundation for such a reaction, some spiritual foundation for such a reaction. What is this reaction? You can't brush it aside. It's a reality, it's there. People are deeply moved by it.

I can only come to this answer. You see, Russia invaded Afghanistan for political motives and certain economic motives. Those people who got in the way were fought and killed. They killed, you could say, the body, but they did not deny the humanity of the individual. In South Africa, what is actually happening, and I think what people sense, is that divine spark I talked about in the human being, the individuality, that which is equal in all human beings, is denied. The core of the individual is denied. So you try to destroy the divine nature of the human being and that is worse than the death of the body. That is the only answer I've been able to come to.

People today, young people of today, perceive that, and this would not have happened even a hundred years ago. Even fifty years ago, that would not have happened. When I look back, for instance, to earlier times, hearing my father speak, who was an extremely gentle man, a very humble man, and yet when I heard him speak in the early days about black people, he spoke quite matter-of-factly. He would not recognize this problem. Yet now, people do. What lies behind it? Something is awakening in human beings, and one needs to see these phenomena. People are beginning to see the other human being in a different light and that's immensely important, but can it come about?

If you look in the Middle East, you see in many areas of the Middle East that something is happening in quite the opposite direction, that denies the individual. A few years ago, when one spoke to the same young people about China, a quite different look came into the eye—a much warmer look. It was totally different. At that time, eight to nine years ago, it was still very much communist, very much a totalitarian state. But people who'd been there, reporters and a certain one or two people I knew who'd been there, confirmed the same thing. In China, although the individual was in a certain sense denied (you weren't expected to have your own opinion, and you had to accept the common opinion), still you were recognized as one of the family.

That whole aspect which arises when we talked about the cultural life, the unique individual, in China, in a certain sense, is denied. But you were recognized as one of the family, one of the people. There was an element of brotherhood, a feeling of brotherhood. I found this extraordinary in such a totalitarian state, that this feeling of brotherhood should be so dominant. That is what many young people sensed, and that, I think, was one of the shocks of the recent repression of the pro-democracy movement. Even the army, who had been looked on as brothers, suddenly turned on their own people, and that was a deep, deep shock that in a way reverberated around the world.

Now if we look at what's happening in Eastern Europe and in Russia, it's very difficult to know actually what is happening. The danger is that there's an economic life there in Russia, and in Poland and in one or two places, which will collapse. That could unleash all sorts of destructive forces and the whole thing could go wrong. We don't know what could happen. But if the economic life collapses, the whole thing could go into reverse. It's very important that this doesn't happen.

But what lives in a person like Gorbachev, and in his foreign minister, Schevardnadsy? Gorbachev is a very interesting man; actually his mother was Roman Catholic. He still had elements of and a certain connection with religion as a child. I find it very interesting, and one doesn't again know why, but he doesn't deny communism. He still feels that the Communist Party has a proper role to play, that it should be dominant. He doesn't want to bring democracy into the whole at the moment. That to me is a question. What lies behind that? Is it purely political? It could be. I have a sneaking suspicion it might be something more. I think it's a great mistake to think that Russia and East Europe are merely going to become similar to the Western states. That is the other danger.

One danger is that the economy will collapse, and it reverts to some form of totalitarianism which would create untold poverty. The other danger is it merely becomes a copy of the West. I feel what is trying to emerge in a perhaps unconscious way is something new—something of the nature of threefoldness. You see, democracy does not belong to the whole of social life. Democracy has its rightful place in that area where you could say every human being's opinion is of equal value—the realm of the state, the realm of law. There democracy has its proper place. But, for instance, in the realms of education, of religion, of science, of medicine, democracy does not have its proper place. Democracy does not belong there. You can't arrive at how to heal a person by taking a vote on it in the general population.

In our cultural-spiritual life, that where our imagination, our creative abilities lie, there we have to find some entirely other way of arriving at decision and of guiding that, and democracy must be kept out of it. In a different way, the same is true of economic life. I wonder whether Gorbachev senses this. Perhaps not a communist party, but for cultural life we have to find a form of people working together which doesn't depend on democracy.

Some years ago when I had a study group at Emerson, I had a very interesting man, a young German there. He took a term off, soon after the Czechoslovakian uprising, about fifteen years ago, in what is known as the Prague Spring. He took a bit of time to study it after it had been suppressed. He really looked to see what was happening, and he came to a startling perception: What they were trying to do there was actually to separate these three spheres.

The realm of the state, democracy, was really trying to be separated so it would not make decisions that affected the cultural-spiritual life. To really try to free the cultural-spiritual life. Economic life, within a framework dictated by the state, within a framework of safety of pollution, and so on, would have to make its own decisions. I was immensely interested. We all were. We could see that something was trying to come there. In Czechoslovakia, they stated quite categorically they were not denying communism nor did they want the forms of the West. They wanted something that was in between.

So something is ready to be born there. Something is trying to come about. The question is, will it be able to? Are the people and the thoughts there that are capable of taking hold of these ideas? After World War I, China tried to bring something about, but the old thoughts took hold again and the opportunity was missed. There were times after World War II when there was the possibility for new things to come about, but they didn't happen then. There were some very interesting people (look at some of the finances and some of ideas that came about), but they didn't quite make the whole. Therefore much of it had a certain health for a while and then began to deteriorate, and we're in that same situation now.

Much of what can happen in the future—whether there are ideas in the future, whether there is the imagination to deal with theses things in the future, whether the thoughts are living—I think much of that will come back to our schools. How are the children educated and what are they educated for?

Rudolf Steiner pointed to the fact that the young child up to the age of seven is an imitative being. The young child up to the age of seven imitates what's going on around him, imitates the parents, everything he sees, and it's very important that the child can and does imitate that which is healthy to imitate. Only the child that imitates, that goes through a healthy imitation up to this age of seven, will as a adult come to a perception of freedom, an understanding of the nature of freedom. Between the age of 7 and 14, that is an age when the children really need to meet a certain form of authority. The authority that compels one to do that which has to be done, that which is right. It's very important that they experience the authority to do what is right, what has to be done, because only if they experience that at that age do they as adults come to an understanding of the equality of people, the equality of individuals, this whole realm of equality.

Then from the age of 14 to 21, it's important that they come to meet other people, that they come to meet the world. They go out into the world and have a certain meeting with the world, and they develop, you could say, a love for the world. Not only a physical love, but a love for their fellow people. Many of them are ready to do this, and this should be encouraged and enabled, because only then will they as adults come to a true sense of brotherhood. These are three things which are longed for in this world today, and which many are struggling for. Answers to the questions of equality, of freedom, and of brotherhood are being searched for.

There are many people out there in the world, many individualities in business, in the trade unions, in government, in city council—leaders who are looking for something. I've heard the expression that they've tried all the old ways of thinking to arrive at conclusions in dealing with social questions, and none of them work. They've got to find a new way of thinking. I've heard that expression. How do we arrive at a new way of thinking? Many of these people would understand something like the threefold nature of social life if it were brought in their language— if it were brought in a practical way, not with any philosophy behind it, but in ordinary everyday language, because it's real; it is out there. Many of them perceive bits of it, and they're waiting for new ideas. I'm quite convinced of it.

So much rests on our schools—that these ideas live in the schools. They will not live in the schools if it merely rests in the teaching, in the classroom, and if the rest is a lie. I'll put it as strongly as that. If only in the classroom is the real spiritual work done, and in the rest are just the old forms of thought—the old ways, the ways of the world which so often are going wrong—then it will not work. So a great task lies on the teachers, on the administrators and the whole school staff; and I would say in respect to the schools, I think the parents can play a great part in this. To warm that community, to support the work, to take it up, and really to demand that that spirituality goes all the way through, the parents can help.

I'd like to finish by leaving you with a certain thought. Only a little while ago, I was at a concert and we were listening to Beethoven's "Choral" Symphony (*Symphony No. 9 in D minor*), a beautiful work. It was in the Festival Hall in London which holds 3000–4000 people. When I looked around, I found myself full of questions: What was the moment I was living? What was this whole situation? This tremendous music resounded through the hall. What was that music? Think of it: 3000–4000 people had come to listen to this music. They could have bought a recording of it for less than the cost of the ticket and listened to it in the comfort of their own home, but they hadn't. They'd come to hear it live. The music resounded through that hall. Then one looks at the faces of the individuals, of the people, and asks the questions: What lives in each person? Who is that person? What do they hear? What speaks to them? What speaks to them out of that music?

I remember another occasion in a very similar situation and that time it was Handel's *Messiah*. I remember that aria out of the *Messiah*, "I know that my redeemer liveth." It was sung by that soloist standing there, the soloist standing there singing those words with the sound ringing out. What did each person hear? Were they conscious of what they were hearing? Did they know what they were listening to? What was their experience? I think we sometimes fail to ask the questions. As we go through life, as we look at these things, we fail to ask the questions, and the questions are always the first part of the answer. Without the question, without learning to question what we see, to question what's living there, to question who are you, we'll never come to recognition of what's around us. We have to learn to question and to observe. We come to many beautiful ideas that live in our heads, but which don't really stand up if we observe what's going on in life and if we ask these questions. So, I'd like to leave you with this thought: Learn to ask the questions.

Endnotes

1   This information was taken from *Die Entfaltung der Idee der Waldorfschule im Summer 1919* [The Unfolding of the Idea of the Waldorf School in the Summer of 1919] by E.A. Karl Stockmeyer, as printed in the 70th Anniversary edition *Erziehungskunst*.

2   From *Anthroposophy and the Social Question* (1905) by Rudolf Steiner. "In a community of human beings working together, the well being of the community will be the greater, the less the individual claims for himself the proceeds of the work he himself has done. In other words, the more of these proceeds he makes over to his fellow workers, the more his own requirements are satisfied, not out of his own work done, but out of the work done by others."